WHERE PEOPLE LIVE

LIFE IN THE COUNTRYSIDE

WRITTEN BY
Noah Leatherland

KidHaven PUBLISHING

Published in 2025 by
KidHaven Publishing, an Imprint of
Greenhaven Publishing, LLC
2544 Clinton St., Buffalo, NY 14224

Written by: Noah Leatherland
Edited by: Rebecca Phillips-Bartlett
Designed by: Jasmine Pointer

Cataloging-in-Publication Data

Names: Leatherland, Noah, 1999-.
Title: Life in the countryside / Noah Leatherland.
Description: Buffalo, NY : KidHaven Publishing, 2025. | Series: Where people live | Includes glossary and index.
Identifiers: ISBN 9781534549197 (pbk.) | ISBN 9781534549203 (library bound) | ISBN 9781534549210 (ebook)
Subjects: LCSH: Country life--Juvenile literature.
Classification: LCC GT3470.L38 2025 | DDC 307.72--dc23

Manufactured in the United States of America

CPSIA compliance information: Batch #CW25KH
For further information contact Greenhaven Publishing LLC at 1-844-317-7404.

Please visit our website, www.greenhavenpublishing.com.
For a free color catalog of all our high-quality books, call toll free 1-844-317-7404 or fax 1-844-317-7405.

Find us on

IMAGE CREDITS

All images are courtesy of Shutterstock.com. With thanks to Getty Images, Thinkstock Photo and iStockphoto.
Cover – HappyPictures, Picksell, Lena Platonova, PIYATHILAKA. Alien Character – HappyPictures. Background throughout – Picksell. 4–5 – NicoElNino, Lena Platonova, MaxyM. 6–7 – Ruslana Iurchenko, SNEHIT PHOTO. 8–9 – JSvideos, Olezzo. 10–11 – Leena Robinson, Lena Platonova, Anne Kitzman, Richard Cavalleri, Julian Worker. 12–13 – Jacob Lund, Pressmaster. 14–15 – Leigh Trail, Monkey Business Images, Katya Kandalova. 16–17 – Rob Hainer, Monkey Business Images. 18–19 – Monkey Business Images, 4 PM production. 20–21 – Budimir Jevtic, Visionsi. 22–23 – John Couture, 19 STUDIO, HappyPictures.

CONTENTS

WORDS THAT LOOK LIKE **THIS** CAN BE FOUND IN THE GLOSSARY ON PAGE 24.

WELCOME TO EARTH

Hello to all my viewers on Morpia. My name is Morp. Welcome back to a new episode of Where People Live – the show that looks at Earth and all the humans who live there.

Humans live on nearly every part of Planet Earth. They live in hot places, cold places, and everywhere in between. They build all sorts of **SETTLEMENTS**. Today, we will be exploring settlements in the countryside.

WHAT HUMANS MEAN

SETTLEMENTS: Anywhere that a group of people builds a place to live

WHAT ON EARTH IS THE COUNTRYSIDE?

While some settlements have lots of buildings and many humans living there, the countryside is almost the opposite. The countryside is the RURAL space away from big settlements and close to nature.

WHAT HUMANS MEAN

RURAL: To do with the open land away from towns and cities

Humans might spread out in the countryside and live away from other humans. Sometimes, they live in little settlements, such as villages. Villages have a much smaller **POPULATION** than cities.

WHAT HUMANS MEAN

POPULATION: How many people live in a place

WHERE ARE THEY GOING?

You might see some humans who live in the countryside heading towards the towns and cities. There are usually more jobs in bigger settlements. So, people in the countryside **COMMUTE** for work.

WHAT HUMANS MEAN

COMMUTE: To travel to a job

You might also see some humans from the cities heading to the countryside. They might be **TOURISTS**. They are coming to visit the countryside to have some fun and relax.

WHAT HUMANS MEAN

TOURISTS: People who visit another place for fun

WHAT IS IN THE COUNTRYSIDE?

After taking a look around the countryside, I came across some very interesting places. Here are a few things that I saw.

Humans who belong to a **religion** use these places to **pray** and **worship**.

PLACES OF WORSHIP

FARMS

RANCHES

Ranches are big farms that have a lot of animals.

STORES

HOUSES

HAVING FUN IN THE COUNTRYSIDE

Humans like to have fun in their free time. Although places in the countryside might not have as many FACILITIES as cities, humans have a lot of fun in all of the open space.

WHAT HUMANS MEAN

FACILITIES: Places, buildings, and equipment needed for certain activities

Humans spend time in nature. They like to go on long walks. Humans call this hiking. Some humans like to go to places where there is water. They often visit rivers and lakes to catch fish.

SHOPPING IN THE COUNTRYSIDE

Stores are places where humans go to buy things. Places in the countryside do not usually have many stores because there are not as many people as in the towns and cities.

However, villages do have stores that sell **essential** things, such as food and medicine. In the countryside, humans also buy things from LOCAL farms. Some villages have markets where farmers sell their **produce**.

WHAT HUMANS MEAN

LOCAL: To do with the area near where someone lives

TOWN HALLS

Town halls are places where humans meet. They go there to talk about how their settlements are being run. It gives **RESIDENTS** a chance to talk about what they would like to change.

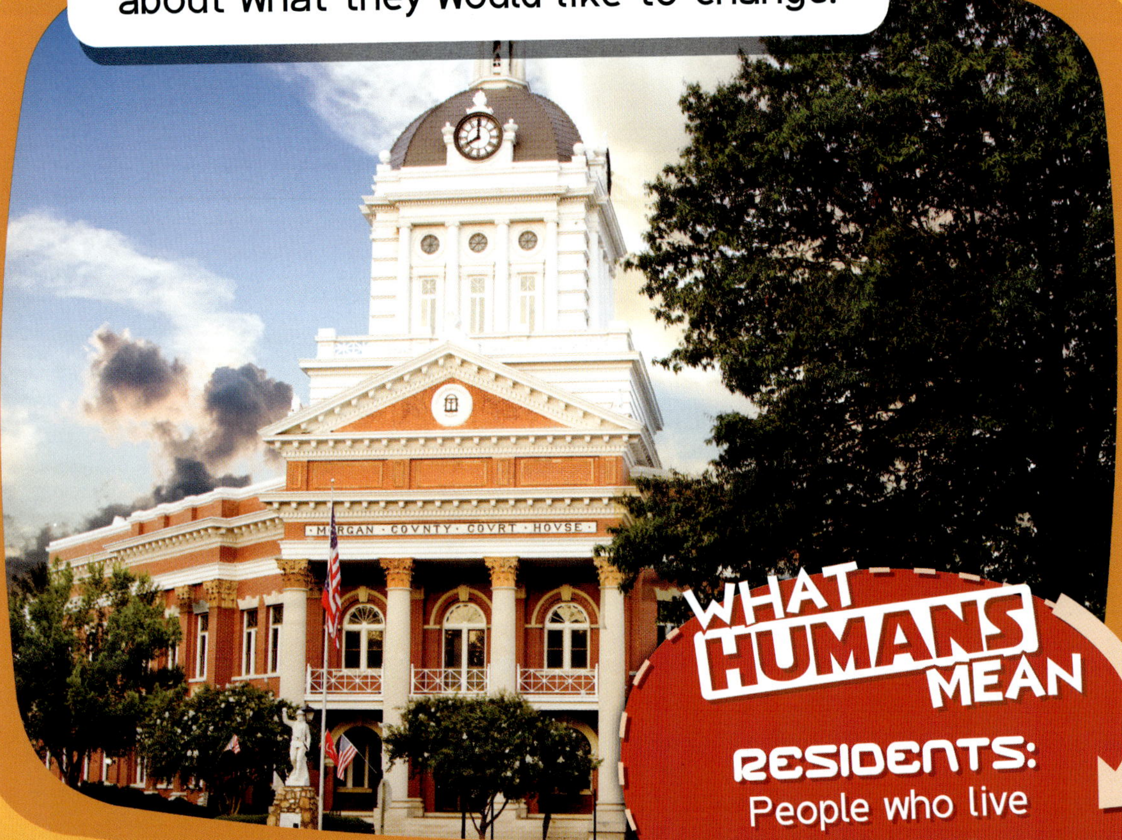

WHAT HUMANS MEAN

RESIDENTS: People who live in an area

In the countryside, some villages might have their own village halls. Others might meet at the town hall of a larger settlement nearby. It gives them an **opportunity** to speak to local leaders.

SCHOOLS

Take a look! Those small humans are called children. They are at school. Villages in the countryside usually have a school for the children who live there.

When the children get older, they might need to go to a school in a nearby town. School buses take children to their school if it is too far for them to walk.

BUSINESSES IN THE COUNTRYSIDE

Businesses are important to human settlements. They give people jobs and bring money in from other places. Businesses in the countryside are different from businesses in bigger settlements.

AGRICULTURE is an important business in the countryside. Some farms focus on growing fruits, vegetables, and **grains**. Others focus on keeping farm animals, such as pigs, cows, and chickens.

WHAT HUMANS MEAN

AGRICULTURE: To do with farming

TUNE IN NEXT WEEK

Well, viewers, there is so much to see in the countryside. Just because some humans like to live far away from big settlements does not mean there is nothing around them.

Humans keep themselves connected to each other. Settlements big and small are connected by roads, rivers, and railways. The countryside could be a lovely home… if you are a human!

GLOSSARY

ESSENTIAL needed for something that cannot be completed without it

GRAINS seeds and fruits of certain plants, such as wheat and rice

NATURE everything in the world that is not made by people

OPPORTUNITY a chance to do something

OPPOSITE completely different

PRAY to talk to a god or gods of a chosen belief

PRODUCE things grown on farms

RELIGION an organized set of beliefs usually centered around a god or gods

WORSHIP a religious act where a person expresses praise for a god or gods

INDEX